Have fun with

Arts and Crafts

Dinosaurs

Rita Storey

W
FRANKLIN WATTS
LONDON • SYDNEY

This edition 2013

First published in 2012 by
Franklin Watts
338 Euston Road
London NW1 3BH

Franklin Watts Australia
Level 17/207 Kent Street
Sydney NSW 2000

Series editor: Amy Stephenson

Packaged for Franklin Watts by Storeybooks
rita@storeybooks.co.uk
Designer: Rita Storey
Editor: Nicola Barber
Crafts: Rita Storey
Photography: Tudor Photography, Banbury
www.tudorphotography.co.uk

A CIP catalogue record for this book is available
from the British Library.

Printed in China

Dewey classification:745.5

ISBN 978 1 4451 2696 8

Cover images: Tudor Photography, Banbury

Franklin Watts is a division of Hachette Children's Books,
an Hachette UK company
www.hachette.co.uk

Before you start

Some of the projects in this book require scissors, paint,
glue, an oven, a kitchen knife and pins. When using
these things we would recommend that children
are supervised by a responsible adult.

Contents

Spotosaur

Dinosaurs lived on Earth millions of years ago. They came in all shapes and sizes. This zany model dinosaur has a round body and colourful spots. It also has a row of spines on its back just like a Stegosaurus.

For a model dinosaur you will need

- balloon
- 2 sheets of A4 paper
- masking tape
- scissors
- 4 strips of thin card 5cm x 10cm
- small pieces of thin card
- 1 tissue
- PVA glue and mixing pot
- paintbrush
- sheets of newspaper torn into small pieces
- yellow paint
- coloured tissue paper
- coin and jar lid to draw round
- 2 googly eyes
- felt-tip pen

1 Blow up the balloon to the size of a small football. Tie a knot in the end.

2 Roll one of the sheets of A4 paper into a tight cone shape. Tape it closed using masking tape.

3 Measure 14cm along your cone from the pointed end and trim off the open end of the cone to create a base with a straight edge. Follow steps 2 – 3 with the other sheet of A4 paper.

4 For the tail, place one of the cones over the knot on the balloon and tape in place with four pieces of masking tape. Attach the other cone in the same way on the opposite side of the balloon to make the neck.

5 To make the legs, roll a strip of thin card into a tube. Tape the tube together with masking tape. Repeat with the other three strips of card.

6 Using small pieces of masking tape, lightly attach one pair of legs just below the tail – they should be roughly 3cm apart. Attach the second pair of legs roughly 4cm in front of the first pair – again about 3cm apart. The balloon should now balance on the legs and the tail should be pointing downwards at an angle. If it is wobbly, reposition the legs until it balances. Then add more masking tape to fix the legs in position.

7 To make the dinosaur's spines, copy the templates on page 30 on to the small pieces of thin card. Cut out the spines. Use masking tape to attach the spines to the balloon as shown, on the opposite side to the legs.

8 To make the dinosaur's head, scrunch the tissue into a ball. Use masking tape to tape it to the end of the neck. Mix some PVA glue in a pot with about the same amount of water. Paint pieces of newspaper with the glue and stick them on to the dinosaur. Keep adding the glued paper pieces until the whole shape is covered in three or four layers. Leave the dinosaur to dry.

9 Paint the dinosaur yellow. Leave to dry.

10 Draw round the coin and jar lid onto the tissue paper. You will need about 40 circles. Cut them out and glue them on to the dinosaur.

11 Glue a googly eye on either side of the head. Use the felt-tip pen to draw on a smiley mouth.

This zany dinosaur would make a good pet.

Dinosaur Cards

These cool dinosaur cards are great for giving to friends on their birthday. They would make great dinosaur party invitations, too.

For a Stegosaurus card you will need

- stiff white paper or card 20cm x 20cm
- felt-tip pen
- scissors
- crayons to decorate your card
- googly eye
- glue

For a Triceratops card you will need

- white stiff A4 paper
- felt-tip pens
- scissors
- crayons to decorate your card
- pencil or a paintbrush

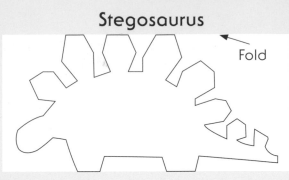

Fold

1 Fold the paper or card in half. Use the template on page 30 to draw a Stegosaurus on the paper as shown. Place the top of the spines against the folded edge of the paper and the feet against the opposite side.

2 Cut out between the spines, taking care not to cut along the folded edge. Cut around the rest of the outline.

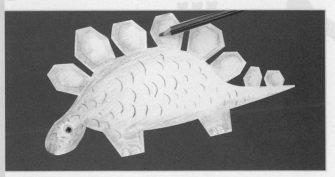

3 Use the crayons to colour the dinosaur. Glue on a googly eye.

Stegosaurus

Stegosaurus was a plant-eater that grew to be the size of a bus. It had plates all along its back and tail. It used its tail to hit other dinosaurs if they attacked it.

Triceratops

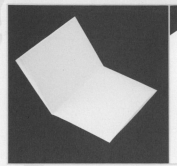
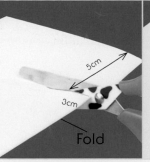
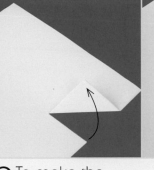
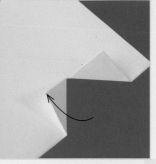

5cm

3cm

Fold

1 Fold the paper in half. Fold the paper in half again the other way. Open out the paper.

2 Fold the paper in half lengthways. Make a 3cm cut at right angles to the fold line 5cm down from the top of the paper as shown.

3 To make the dinosaur's mouth, fold the top corner of the cut paper up. Crease the fold.

4 Fold the bottom corner of the cut paper down. Crease the fold. Fold the corners flat again. Unfold the paper.

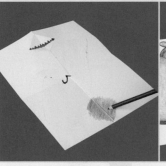
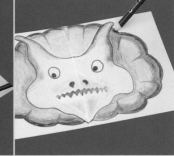

5 To make the teeth, snip a row of triangles out of the paper along both sides of the cut you have made in step 2.

6 At the opposite end of the paper to the mouth, colour in a patch of red as shown. Fold the paper in half so that the mouth is over the patch of red. The mouth will be on the inside of your card.

7 Draw a Triceratops face around the mouth. Remember to add the frill that goes around the Triceratops' neck. Colour it in.

Rrrrrrrrrrrrrrrrrooooooooooooooaaaaaaaaarrrrrr!

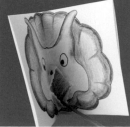

8 Using the end of a pencil or paintbrush, gently pull the cut lines apart along the middle fold. When the card is opened out the mouth of the Triceratops will open in a roar.

Dinostomp

Some dinosaurs were very big. You can feel like a big, scary dinosaur in these brilliant cardboard feet. They are great for stomping around the house or garden. You could make two sets and stomp with a friend.

For dinosaur feet you will need

- tissue paper in shades of green
- PVA glue and mixing pot
- paintbrush
- 2 empty tissue boxes bigger than your feet
- red paper
- yellow paper
- scissors
- pencil

1 Cut or tear the tissue paper into lots of small pieces. The pieces can be different shapes and sizes.

2 Mix the PVA glue with about the same amount of water. Brush the runny glue on to the boxes and stick pieces of tissue paper on to the outside of the box. Use different shades of green to make it look like dinosaur skin.

3 Keep sticking on tissue paper pieces until the boxes are completely covered and so that any writing on the boxes does not show through.

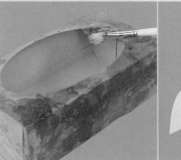

4 Paste a few pieces of tissue paper over the edges of the boxes to tidy them up. Leave the boxes to dry.

5 Using the template on page 30, cut out six toes from the yellow paper.

6 Using the template on page 30, cut out six toenails from the red paper.

7 Using some undiluted PVA glue, glue a red toenail on to each toe. Leave to dry.

8 Glue three toes on to a short end of each box so that they stick out over the edge.

9 Use a pencil to curl the toes down over the end of the box. Put the boxes on your feet and stomp like a dinosaur!

If you have some green tights or socks, put on a pair to make your legs match your cool dinosaur feet.

Imagine you are an enormous dinosaur looking for your next meal!

Dinosaur Disguise

Disguise yourself as a scary dinosaur in this brilliant dinosaur hat. Can you roar like a dinosaur too?

For a dinosaur hat you will need

- compass
- ruler
- felt-tip pen
- large sheet of paper or newspaper
- scissors
- green fleece fabric
- dressmaking pins
- purple fleece fabric
- fabric glue
- 4 x 4cm circles of orange felt
- 2 x 4cm circles of purple felt
- 2 x 3cm circles of orange felt
- 2 x 3cm circles of purple felt
- 2 x 7cm circles of white felt
- 2 x 4cm circles of black felt
- safety pin

The 'right side' of the fabric is the best side of the fabric – the 'wrong side' is the other side.

1 Open the compass to 18cm. Draw a circle on the newspaper. Cut it out.

2 Fold the green fleece fabric in half. Pin the newspaper circle on to the fabric.

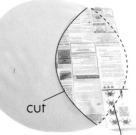

cut

edge of fabric

3 Cut out around the paper circle to make two fleece circles. Unpin the paper circle from the fleece. Lay the two circles of fleece on top of each other with the 'right sides' together.

4 Cut the paper circle in half. Lay a semicircle of paper on top of the two fleece circles. The straight edge should be touching the edges of the circles as shown. Pin in place. Cut round the edge of the newspaper.

5 To make the spines, use the template on page 30. Cut out ten triangles of purple fleece fabric. Paint some glue on to the 'wrong side' of a triangle. Put another triangle on top – the 'wrong sides' should be stuck together. Repeat with the rest of the triangles. Leave to dry.

outer curve

centre seam

6 Spread glue along one edge of each of the spines.

7 Lay a piece of green fleece 'right side up' on a work surface. Stick the spines with the glue along the outer curve as shown. Leave to dry.

8 Spread a centimetre of glue along the edge of the spines nearest the outer curve of the shape. Place the second piece of green fleece on top with the 'right side' down. Pin in place. Leave to dry.

9 To make the teeth, follow steps 5 – 6 using white felt. Open the hat out a little so that the centre seam is facing you and the outer curve is furthest away from you. Glue the teeth on to the inside of the hat in a line across the centre seam. Leave to dry.

Rrrrrrrooooooaaaaaaaaaarrrrrrrrrrrrrrrr.

10 Carefully turn the hat right side out. The spines will stick up out of the top of the hat.

11 Glue the circles of purple and orange felt on to both sides of the hat.

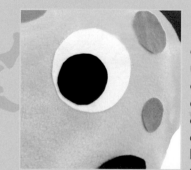

12 For the eyes, glue a circle of white felt half way up the hat – one on each side. Glue a circle of black felt on top of the white circles. Put on the hat. Carefully use the safety pin to pin the bottom points together underneath yor chin.

Pasta Fossil

Dinosaur fossils are marks left by dinosaur skeletons in ancient rocks. Make your own dinosaur fossil picture with pasta shapes and decorate it with sand and glitter.

For a dinosaur fossil you will need

- pencil
- still white card
- pasta shapes
- PVA glue
- paintbrush
- sand
- coloured glitter

1 Draw the outline of a dinosaur fossil on a piece of stiff card. You can make up your own or download one from www.franklinwatts.co.uk

2 Lay the pasta shapes on to the card to make a 3D version of your fossil. Macaroni tubes can be used to draw outlines and to make bones.

3 Spaghetti can be broken into short lengths to make ribs and smaller bones.

4 When you are happy with your fossil you can begin to glue the pasta in place. Pick up a piece of pasta and paint a dab of PVA glue on it.

5 Stick the piece of pasta back on the card in the same place. Repeat until all the shapes are glued in place. Leave to dry.

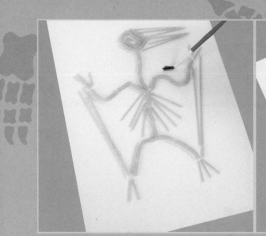
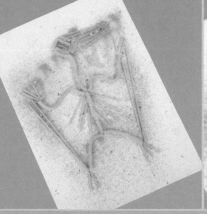
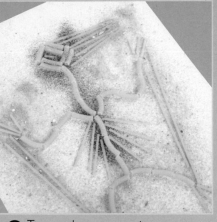

6 Paint the background of the picture with a layer of PVA glue.

7 Sprinkle the sand over the background of the picture. The sand will stick to the background and the dinosaur fossil will show through.

8 To make your picture look really amazing, sprinkle glitter on to some parts of the background. Leave the picture to dry.

Wow! This is the fossil of the fantastic 'sparklosaurus'.

Some dinosaurs were enormous. From the fossilised bones of a Brachiosaurus we can tell that they could have been as big as seventeen elephants and have a neck over 9 metres long!

Fridgeosaur

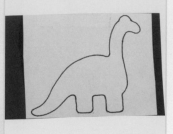

Some dinosaurs had horns, some had scales and some had feathers. These sparkly dinosaurs have glitter and sequins, too. Decorate your own colourful dinosaurs and make a dinosaur scene on your fridge with these great fridge magnets.

For dinosaur fridge magnets you will need

- thin paper
- pencil
- funky foam in green, pink and blue
- masking tape
- ballpoint pen or blunt pencil
- paintbrush
- scissors
- plate
- sequins and feathers
- small magnets
- PVA glue
- googly eyes

1 Trace the Diplodocus template on page 31 on to thin paper.

2 Put the paper on to the pink funky foam. Tape it in place with masking tape.

3 Using a ballpoint pen or blunt pencil, draw round the template. Press hard to make a dent in the foam.

4 Carefully peel off the tape and remove the paper. Draw over the line you have made on the foam. Cut out around the line you have drawn.

5 Paint the dinosaur with a thin layer of PVA glue.

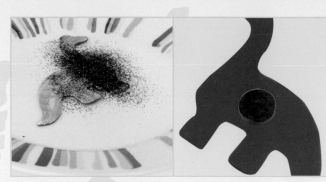

6 Put the dinosaur on to the plate with the glue side up. Sprinkle glitter over the whole dinosaur shape. Leave to dry.

7 When it is dry, tip the excess glitter back on to the plate. Put a blob of glue on a small magnet. Glue it on to the back of the dinosaur. Leave to dry.

8 Decorate the dinosaur with sequins and feathers. Glue on a googly eye. Repeat stages 1 – 7 with the Tyrannosaurus rex template on page 31, but this time use the blue funky foam.

9 Use the templates on page 31 to trace the bush shapes onto thin paper. Follow steps 2 – 4, but this time use the green funky foam. Paint round the curved edge with glue and dust with glitter. Attach a small magnet to the back with a blob of glue. Leave to dry.

These sparkly dinosaurs are nicknamed 'Fridgeosaurs'.

Diplodocus Door Sign

A Diplodocus had a body that was up to 30 metres long and an eight metre neck. They could reach high up into the tallest trees for the juiciest leaves. The long neck of this Diplodocus door sign is just right to hang from a door handle.

To make a Diplodocus door sign you will need

- A4 sheet of stiff purple card
- black felt-tip pen
- scissors
- hole punch
- thin blue card 10cm x 21cm
- A5 sheets of thin, coloured paper – dark green, light green and yellow
- 4 or 5 small sheets of coloured paper
- small piece of coloured card

1 Use the template on page 31 to draw a Diplodocus on to a piece of stiff purple card.

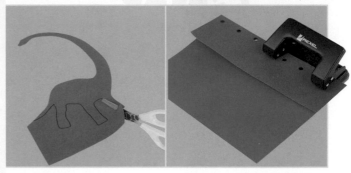

2 Cut around the outline.

3 To make spots for your dinosaur, first empty the hole punch tray. Replace the tray and then punch lots of holes in the small sheets of coloured paper.

4 Empty out the hole punch tray again and glue the small coloured circles you have just made on to the dinosaur to decorate it. Make sure you keep two circles back as they will be your dinosaur's eyes.

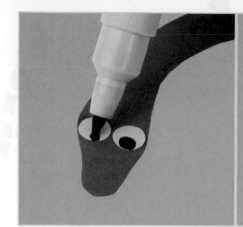  

5 For the eyes, glue two small circles on to the head. Draw a black dot in each circle.

6 Use the templates on page 32 to cut out leaves from the dark green, light green and yellow paper. Glue them on to the card as shown. They can overlap the edges a bit.

7 Glue the dinosaur on to the front of the card, leaving the head and neck of the dinosaur sticking out above the top. This is the part that hangs on the door handle.

8 Write your name on the small piece of coloured card and trim it to an oval shape. Glue it in the space at the top of your door sign.

You could write 'Keep out' or 'BEWARE – DINOSAURS' on your sign instead of your name.

Brighten the door to your room with this colourful door sign.

Icarosaurus Glider

This glider, decorated with a picture of an Icarosaurus, will glide through the air and back into your hand.

For an Icarosaurus glider you will need

- thin paper or tracing paper
- thin white card
- pencil
- masking tape
- crayons
- paintbrush
- glitter glue

You can download a picture of an Icarosaurus to copy from www.franklinwatts.co.uk, or look for one in your school library.

1 Copy the template on page 31 on to a piece of thin paper or tracing paper.

2 Place the paper on to the thin white card. Tape it in place with masking tape. Draw round the shape again, pressing quite hard with the pencil.

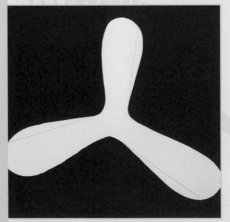

3 Remove the thin paper and masking tape. Cut out the shape on the card following the indented line created in step 2. Your glider should have three equally-sized handles.

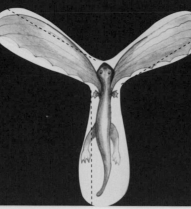

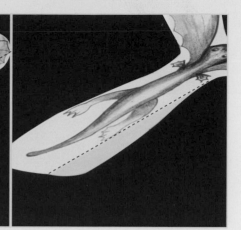

4 Use the crayons to draw an Icarosaurus on the shape. Draw a wing in two of the handles and the body and tail in the third one. Colour it in with the crayons.

5 Draw a dotted line along each handle as shown above.

6 Fold back a small piece of the card along the three dotted lines as shown. This will help the glider to spin in the air and fly back to you.

7 Decorate the glider with glitter glue.

Watch the Icarosaurus spin, then turn and glide back to you.

8 To throw the glider, hold one point in between your finger and thumb. Bend your wrist back. Flick your arm and wrist forward and let go of the glider.

Icarosaurus

Icarosaurus was a small lizard-like dinosaur. It could not fly but it could glide through the air from tree to tree.

Hatching Dinosaur Flip Book

Huge dinosaurs were tiny when they were born. They hatched from eggs, just like birds. Watch a baby dinosaur break out of its egg with this super-animated flip book.

To make a hatching dinosaur flip book you will need

- a small pad of thin paper (glued or stapled at the top – not spiral bound)
- felt-tip pen

The templates for the egg shape and this dinosaur are on page 30.

1 Use the felt-tip pen to draw an egg on the lower half of the last page of the book.

2 Turn over the next page of the book. Trace the egg from the bottom sheet on to the second page. Add a tiny crack at one side of the egg.

Hold the paper up to a bright window to help you trace the picture below.

3 Repeat step 2. Every time you draw the crack in the egg, make it bigger. The more stages you put into a flip book the better, so make the crack only a tiny bit bigger each time.

4 Once the crack has gone right across the egg begin to draw the top of the egg opening up.

5 As the top of the shell opens up, draw the top of a baby dinosaur's head appearing.

6 Then draw the baby dinosaur's eyes.

7 Draw the baby dinosaur's face and arms. Using a green crayon, colour in the dinosaur.

8 Take hold of the pad with your finger at the top and your thumb at the bottom. Lift all the pages up.

9 Let the pages go, one at a time so that you flick from the back of the pad to the front.

10 As you let the pages go the picture will appear to move.

Cccccccccccccccccttttrrrrrraaaaaaacccccckkkkkkkk!

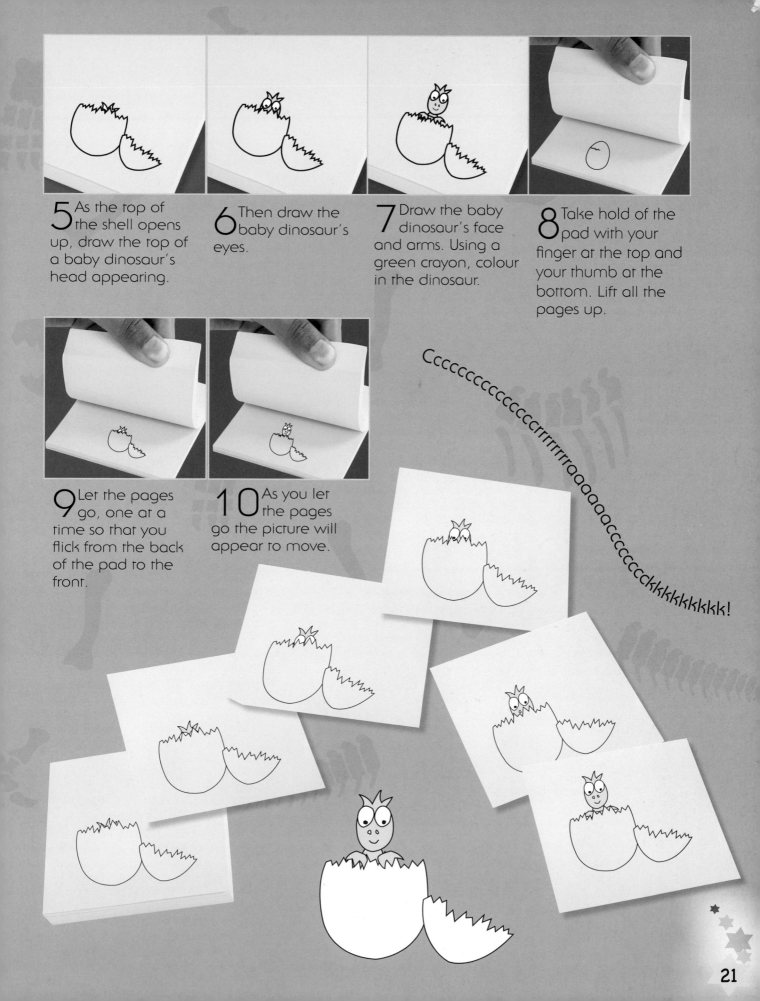

Dinosaur Tooth Necklace

Huge meat-eating dinosaurs such as Tyrannosaurus rex had lots of sharp, deadly teeth. You can make your own dinosaur teeth and string them on to a necklace.

For a dinosaur tooth necklace you will need

- 25g salt
- 50g flour
- bowl
- water
- pastry board
- knife
- paintbrush
- baking tray
- slice
- wire rack
- brown watercolour paint
- necklace cord
- needle with a large eye
- beads

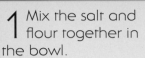

1 Mix the salt and flour together in the bowl.

2 Add water a bit at a time and keep mixing until the dough is very thick and no longer sticky. Make it into a ball. Roll the dough into a long sausage.

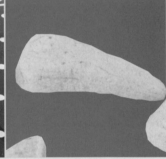

3 Cut off as many small pieces of dough as the number of teeth you want to make. Roll each one into a ball.

4 Shape the ball into the shape of a pointed dinosaur tooth.

5 Use the end of the paintbrush to make a hole right through the tooth shape at the wide end.

Ask an adult to help you bake these salt dough teeth.

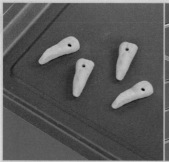

6 Put the teeth on to a baking tray. Bake the teeth in the oven at its lowest (coolest) setting for 2 – 3 hours until the teeth are hard.

7 Use the slice to put the teeth on a wire rack to cool.

8 When the teeth have cooled, mix the watercolour paint with water. Paint the teeth to make them look like real dinosaur teeth. Leave them to dry.

9 Thread the necklace cord through the eye of the needle. Push the needle through the hole in the first tooth.

10 If you want a necklace with lots of teeth, thread more teeth and beads on to the necklace cord to make a pattern.

11 If you want just one tooth on the necklace, thread one bead above it and tie a knot in the necklace cord to stop it slipping.

12 Put the necklace round your neck. Ask an adult to cut the ends of the necklace cord so that the necklace is the length you want it to be, plus some extra to tie. Tie the ends at the back of your neck.

This dough will make about 30 teeth. To use up the rest of the dough you could make a model dinosaur.

Wear your dinosaur tooth necklace to scare off other dinosaurs.

Dinosaur Salad

Not all dinosaurs ate lots of meat – lots of dinosaurs enjoyed their greens too! Make this yummy dinosaur salad picture – it's healthy, too!

For a dinosaur salad you will need

- plate
- lettuce
- 2 slices of salami
- 2 slices of hard-boiled egg
- kitchen knife
- 2 slices of cucumber
- mini pitta bread
- slice of cheddar cheese
- 2 pieces of baby corn
- 2 small carrots
- red pepper
- 2 black olives
- squeezy mayonnaise

1 Lay some pieces of lettuce on the plate. Put two slices of salami side-by-side on top of the lettuce, near the top of the plate.

2 For the eyes, put two slices of hard-boiled egg on top of the salami slices.

3 Put the pitta bread in the middle of the plate slightly overlapping the salami slices. Tuck a piece of cucumber under the pitta bread on either side.

4 To make teeth, cut the cheese slice into triangles. Arrange the triangles at the bottom edge of the pitta bread, with one of the points facing down.

5 Put a second row of cheese triangles along the bottom of the plate with one of the points facing up. Put a baby corn and a small carrot on either side to make sharp fangs.

6 Cut the olives in half. Put half an olive on each hard-boiled egg slice. To make the nostrils, put two olives side-by-side on the middle of the pitta bread.

7 Finish the picture by cutting two half circles of red pepper and putting them above the salami. Squeeze on some mayonnaise hair. Eat up your delicious dinosaur lunch!

To make this into a vegetarian salad, replace the salami with two circles of cheese or two big slices of tomato.

Attack your dinosaur lunch and make it extinct!

Fingerprint Dinosaurs

Get printing to create a whole family of cute fingerprint dinosaurs. You could print them on cards for your friends or make a dinosaur picture to hang in your bedroom.

To make a fingerprint dinosaur you will need

- paint in different colours
- baking tray for each colour paint
- scrap of paper
- sheet of white paper
- felt-tip pen

Tyrannosaurus rex

Tyrannosaurus rex was one of the most fearsome dinosaurs that ever lived. Its strong legs and powerful tail helped it move quickly to catch its prey. It became extinct about 65 million years ago.

Basic Dinosaur Body

1 Squeeze a blob of paint on to a baking tray. Dip your finger in the paint. Make a fingerprint on the scrap paper to remove any excess paint.

2 Make a fingerprint on the sheet of paper. Make more prints, building up an oval shape. This shape will be the body of the dinosaur.

Stegosaurus

1 Make a basic body with green paint. Print two thumbprints sideways at the front of the body to make a neck and a head.

2 Make two fingerprints at the bottom of the body to make legs.

3 Make two prints at the back of the dinosaur for the tail. Make a smaller print using your little finger at the end of the tail.

4 In a different colour, print a line of fingerprints along the top of the body to make spines. Use the felt-tip pen to draw a mouth and a dot for the dinosaur's eye.

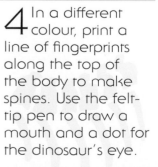

Tyrannosaurus Rex

1 Make a basic body with red paint. Make two prints straight out from the body at the back of the dinosaur for the tail. Make a smaller print, using your little finger, at the end of the tail.

2 Make two fingerprints joined to each other for the neck. Make a larger thumbprint sideways to make the head.

3 Make two thumbprints at the bottom of the body to make the top of the legs.

4 Make two fingerprints joined to each other for the rest of the legs. Make a smaller print, using your little finger, for the foot.

5 Draw a dot near to the top of the head for the eye of the dinosaur. Draw sharp teeth on the head where the mouth would be.

Triceratops Eggcup

This funky Triceratops eggcup will turn a boiled egg into a monster treat. Go wild with some really bright colours and make one for each of your family or friends.

For a Triceratops eggcup you will need

- air-dry clay
- large egg
- clingwrap
- paints
- paintbrushes
- water
- clear varnish (optional)

1 Roll a piece of clay into a long sausage shape. Carefully wrap the egg in clingwrap.

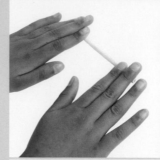

2 Starting at the top, wind the clay sausage round and round the egg in a spiral so that each loop touches the one above. Stop at the widest point of the egg.

3 Break off the remaining sausage of clay and smooth down the broken edge. Remove the egg. This will be the eggcup.

4 To make the triceratops' head, roll a piece of clay into a ball. Shape it into a cone. Flatten the wide end of the cone.

5 Take a piece of clay and press it into a flat pancake shape. Dab a little water on to the flat end of the head. Stick it on to the bottom of the pancake shape as shown.

6 To make a foot, roll three small and one medium-sized pieces of clay into balls. Press the balls together. Repeat to make the other foot.

7 Press the two feet together.

8 Press the cup onto the feet. Press the head onto the front of the cup.

9 To make the tail, roll another ball of clay into a fat sausage. Make it thicker at one end. Attach the thick end to the eggcup on the opposite side to the head. Bend it into an 's' shape.

10 Roll two very small pieces of clay into small cones to make horns. Press them on to the head of the dinosaur near the top.

11 You can paint the dinosaur to look like the one in the picture below, or make up a design of your own. Leave to dry.

To make your eggcup waterproof, paint it with a coat of clear varnish.

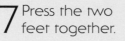

Templates

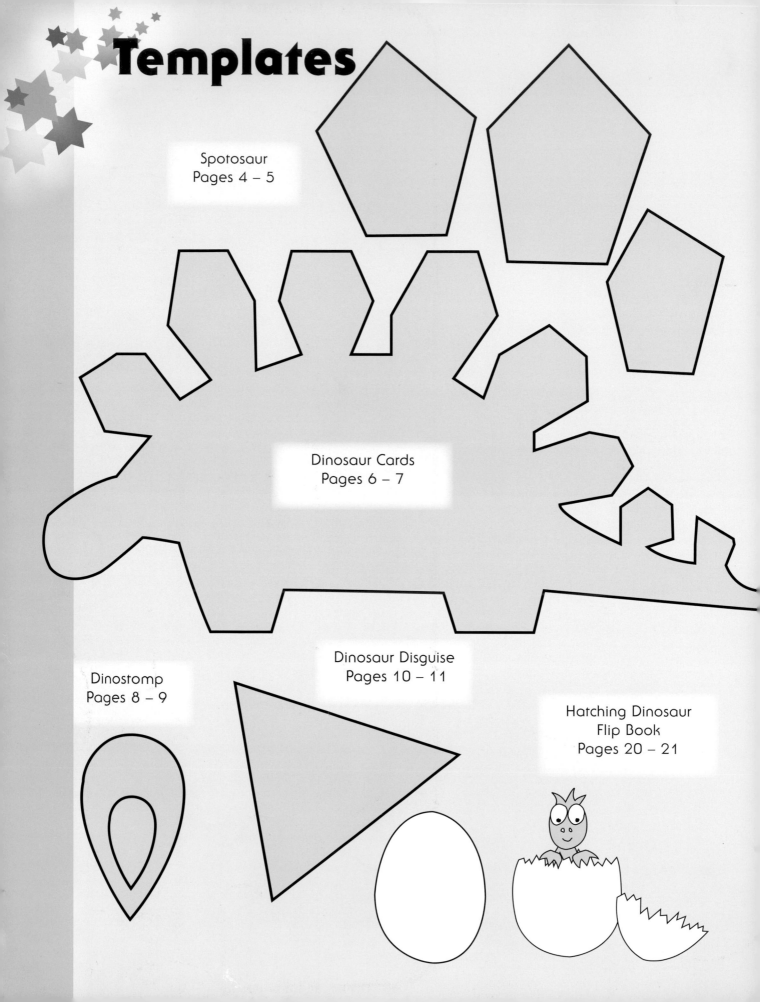

Spotosaur
Pages 4 – 5

Dinosaur Cards
Pages 6 – 7

Dinostomp
Pages 8 – 9

Dinosaur Disguise
Pages 10 – 11

Hatching Dinosaur
Flip Book
Pages 20 – 21

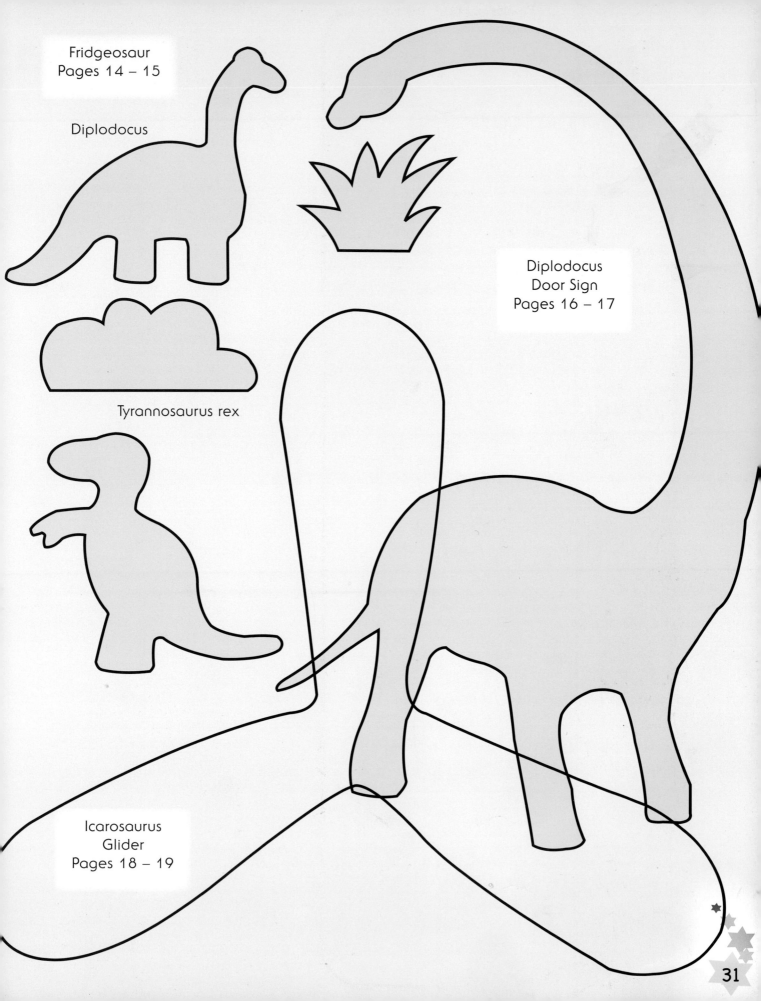

Fridgeosaur
Pages 14 – 15

Diplodocus

Diplodocus
Door Sign
Pages 16 – 17

Tyrannosaurus rex

Icarosaurus
Glider
Pages 18 – 19

Further Information

Diplodocus
Door Sign
Pages 16 – 17

Leaf

Books

Dinosaurs by Joseph Staunton (Franklin Watts, 2012)

Drawing Is Fun: Drawing Dinosaurs by Rebecca Clunes, Lisa Mile and Trevor Cook (Franklin Watts, 2012)

Prehistoric Safari: series by Liz Miles (Franklin Watts, 2013)

Dinosaurs!: series by David West (Franklin Watts, 2013)

Websites

http://www.nhm.ac.uk/kids-only/dinosaurs/

http://www.thecolor.com/Category/Coloring/Dinosaur.aspx

http://www.dinosaurfacts.org/

Index